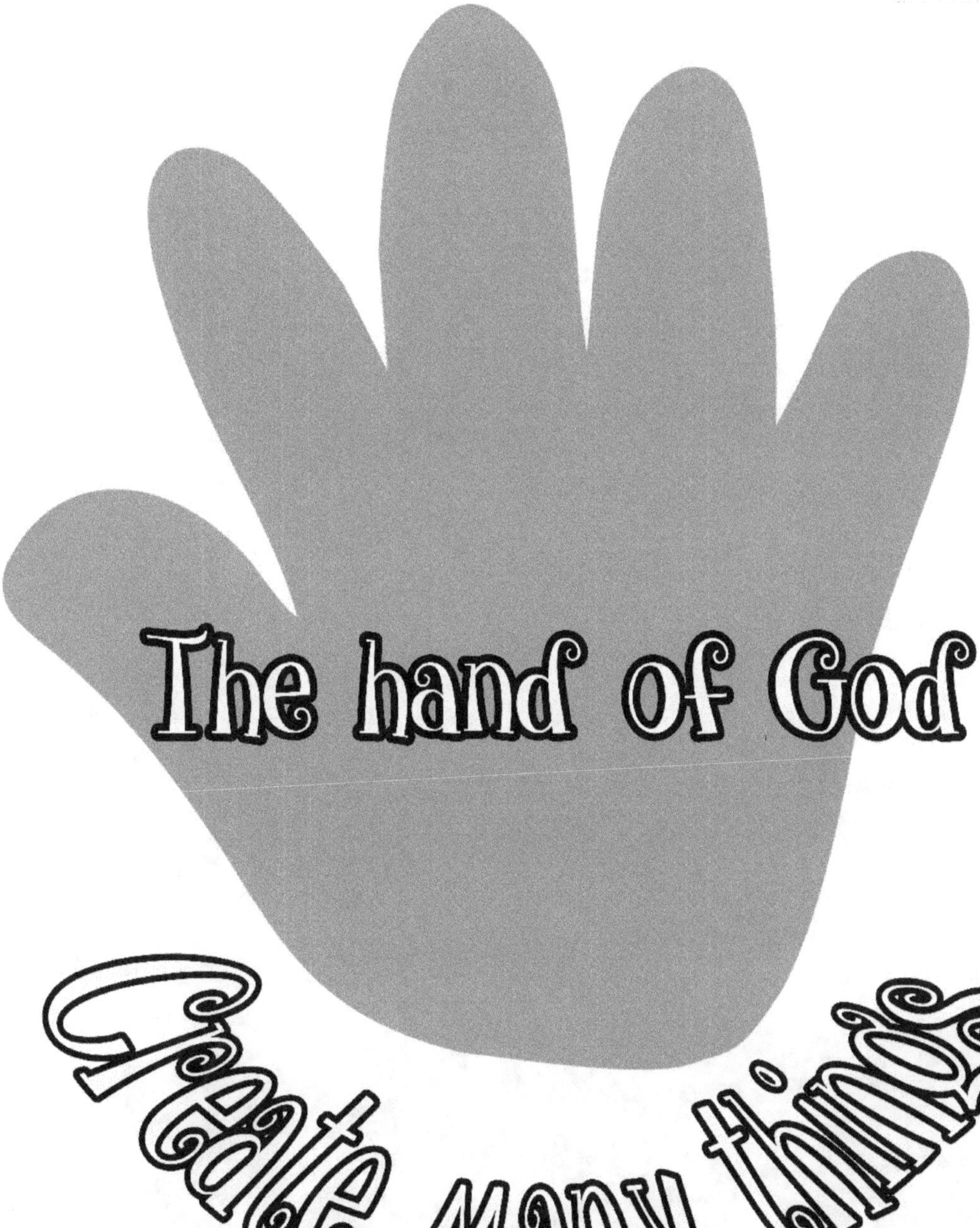

Create many things.

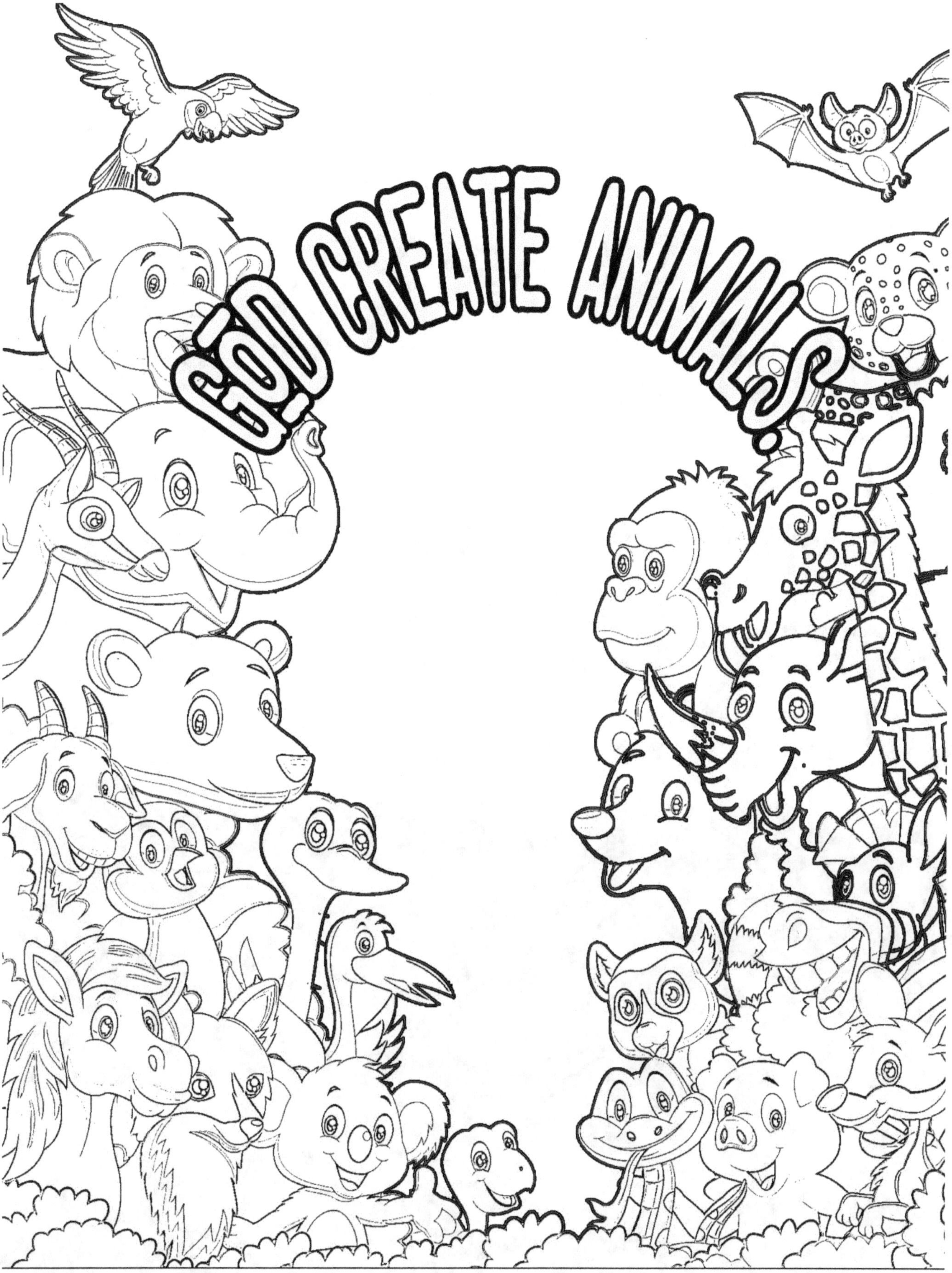
GOD CREATE ANIMALS

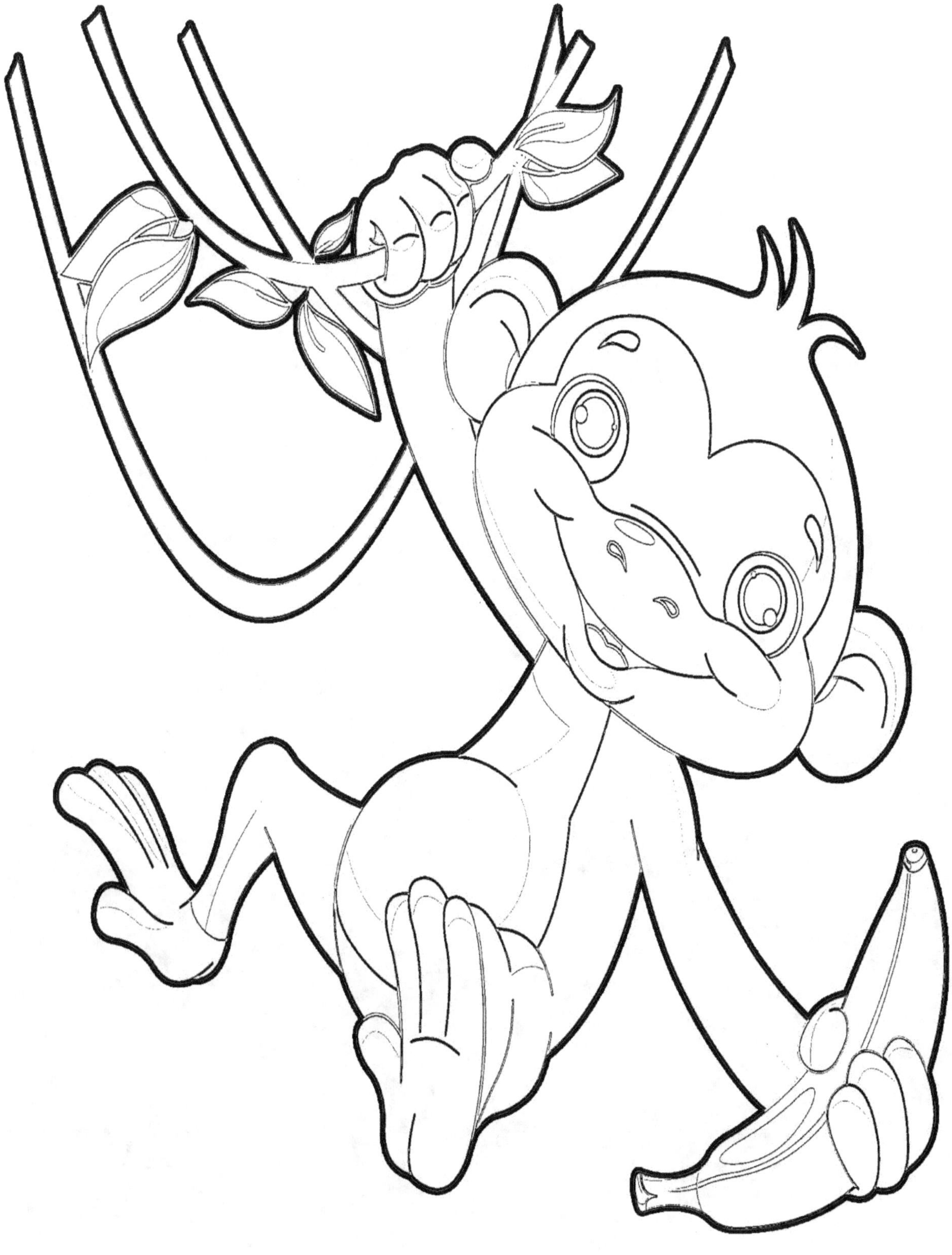

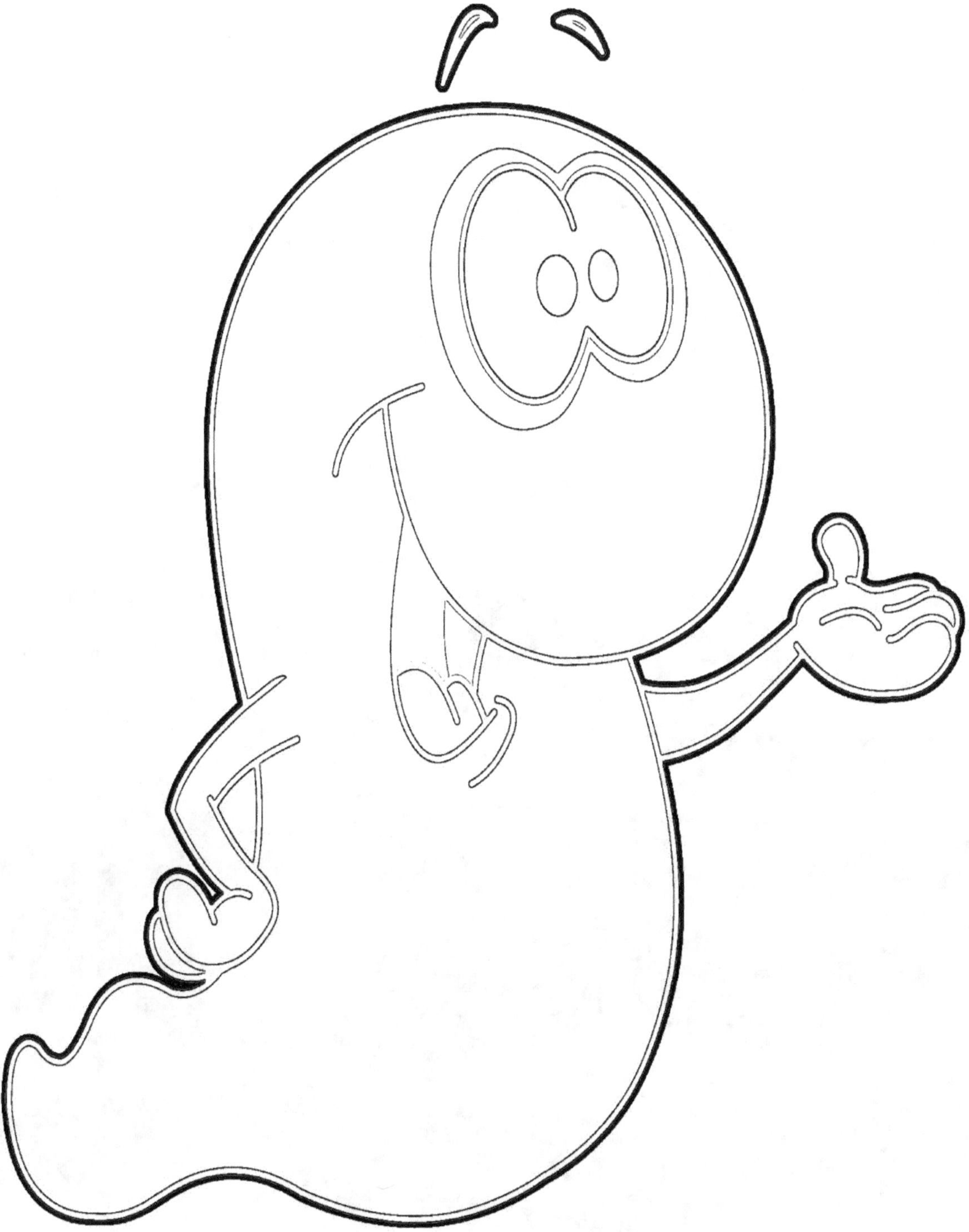

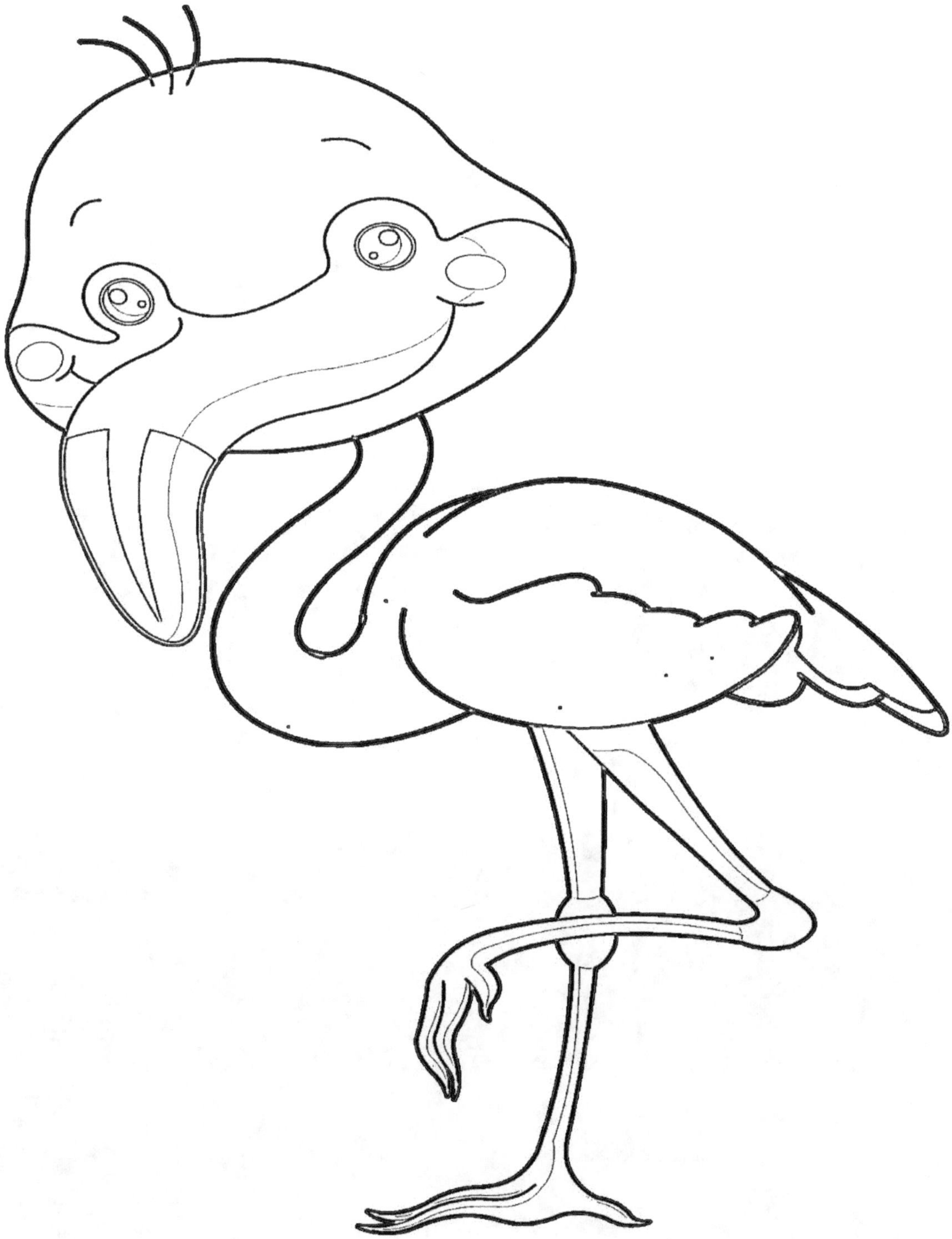

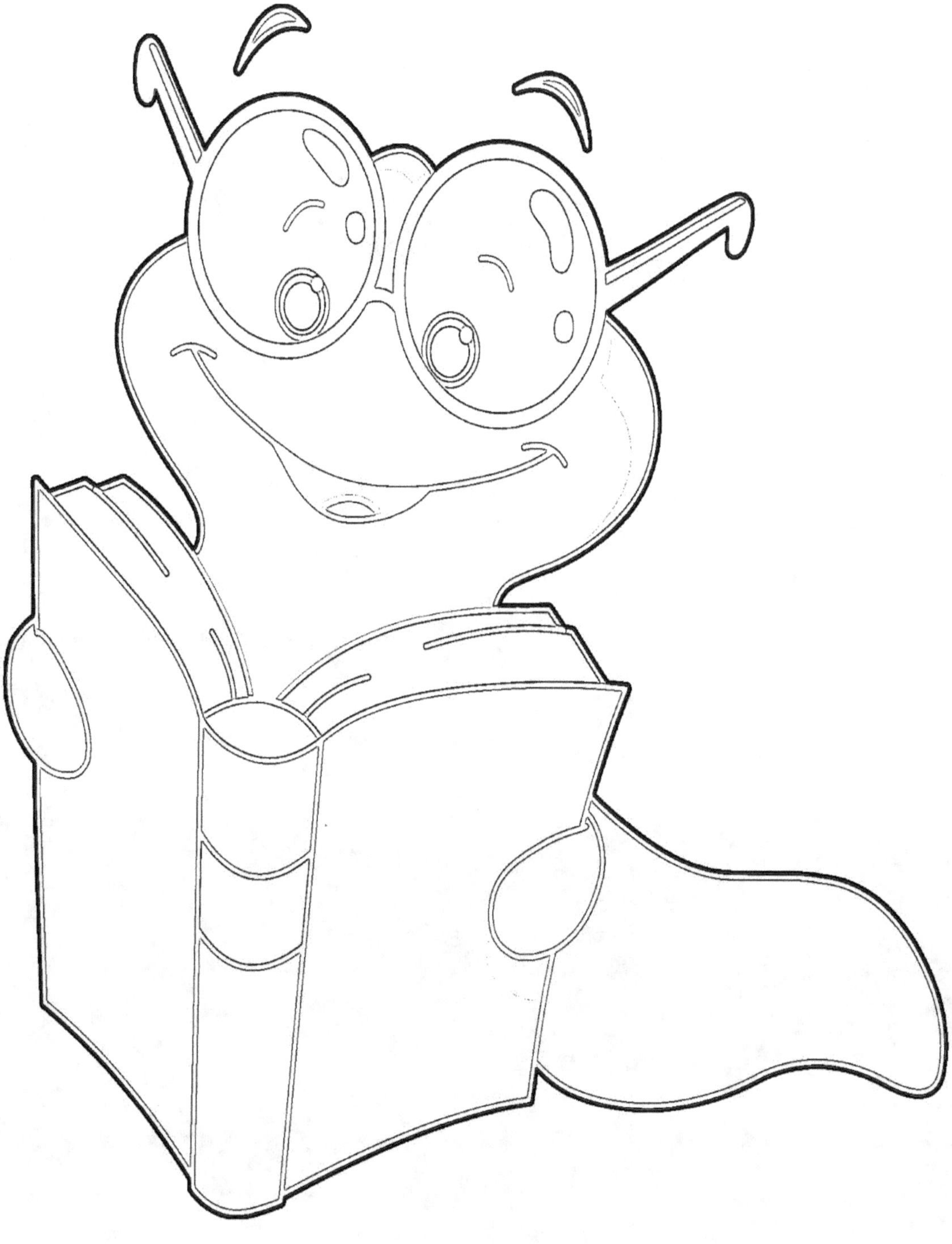

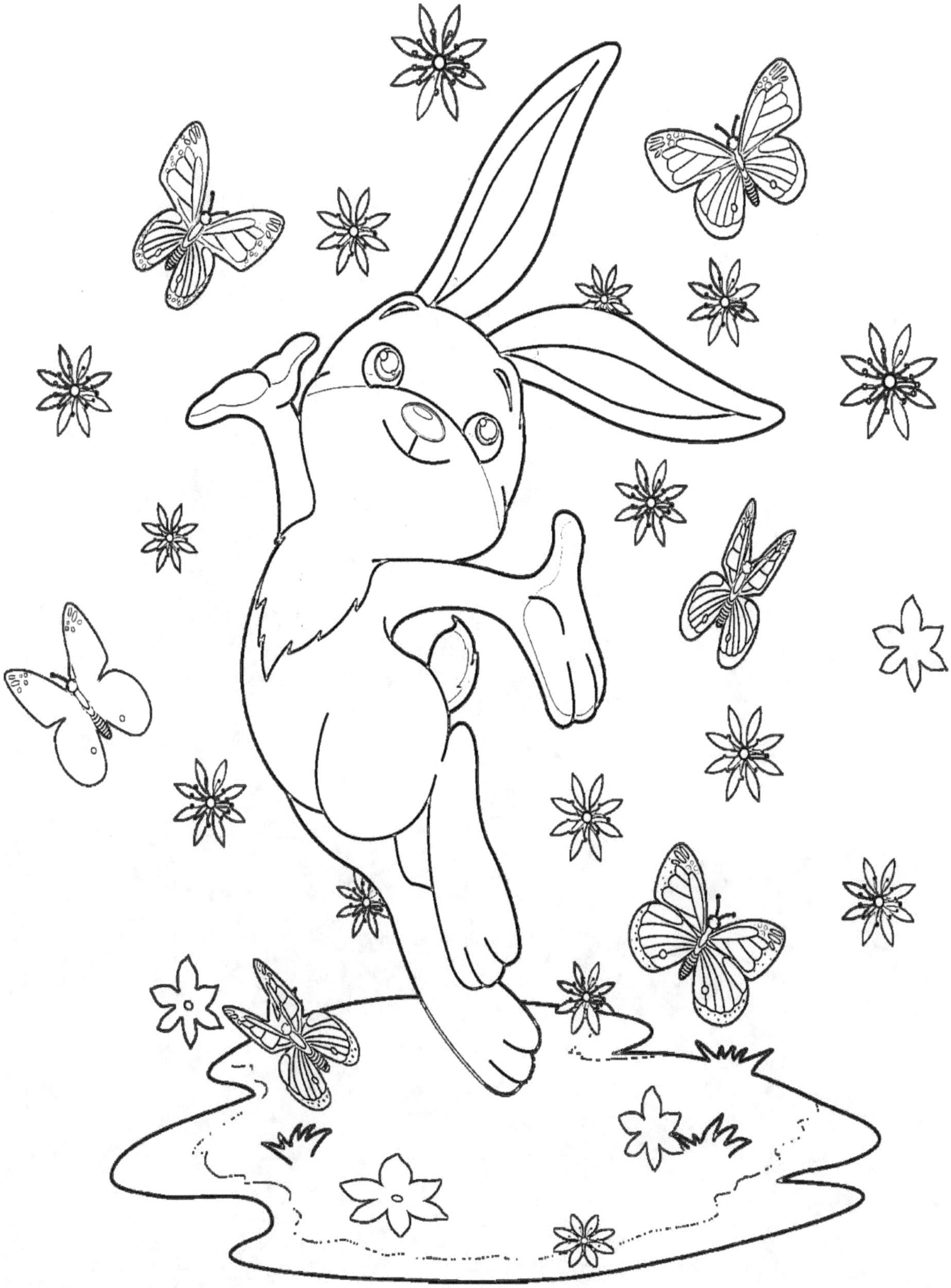

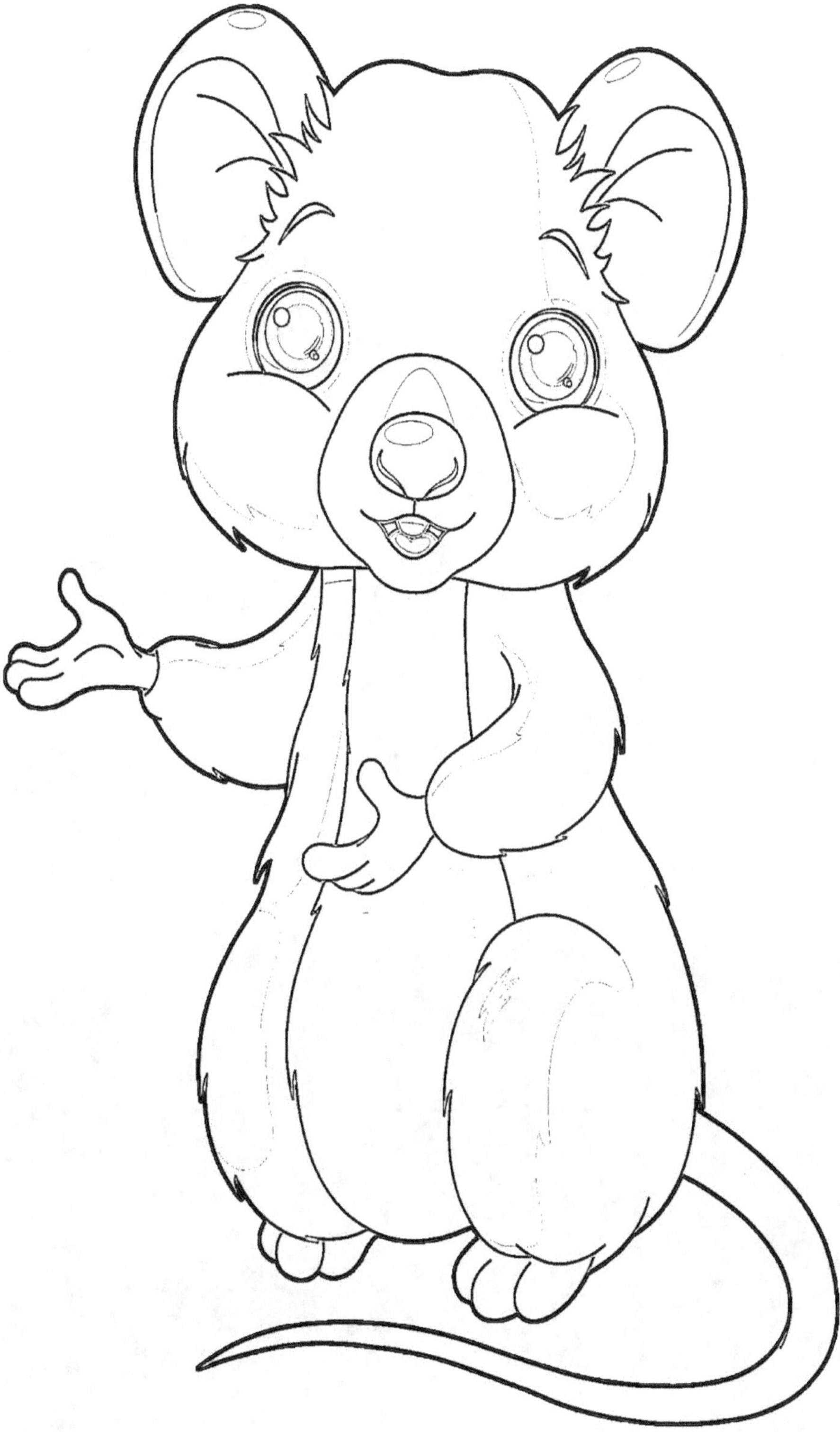

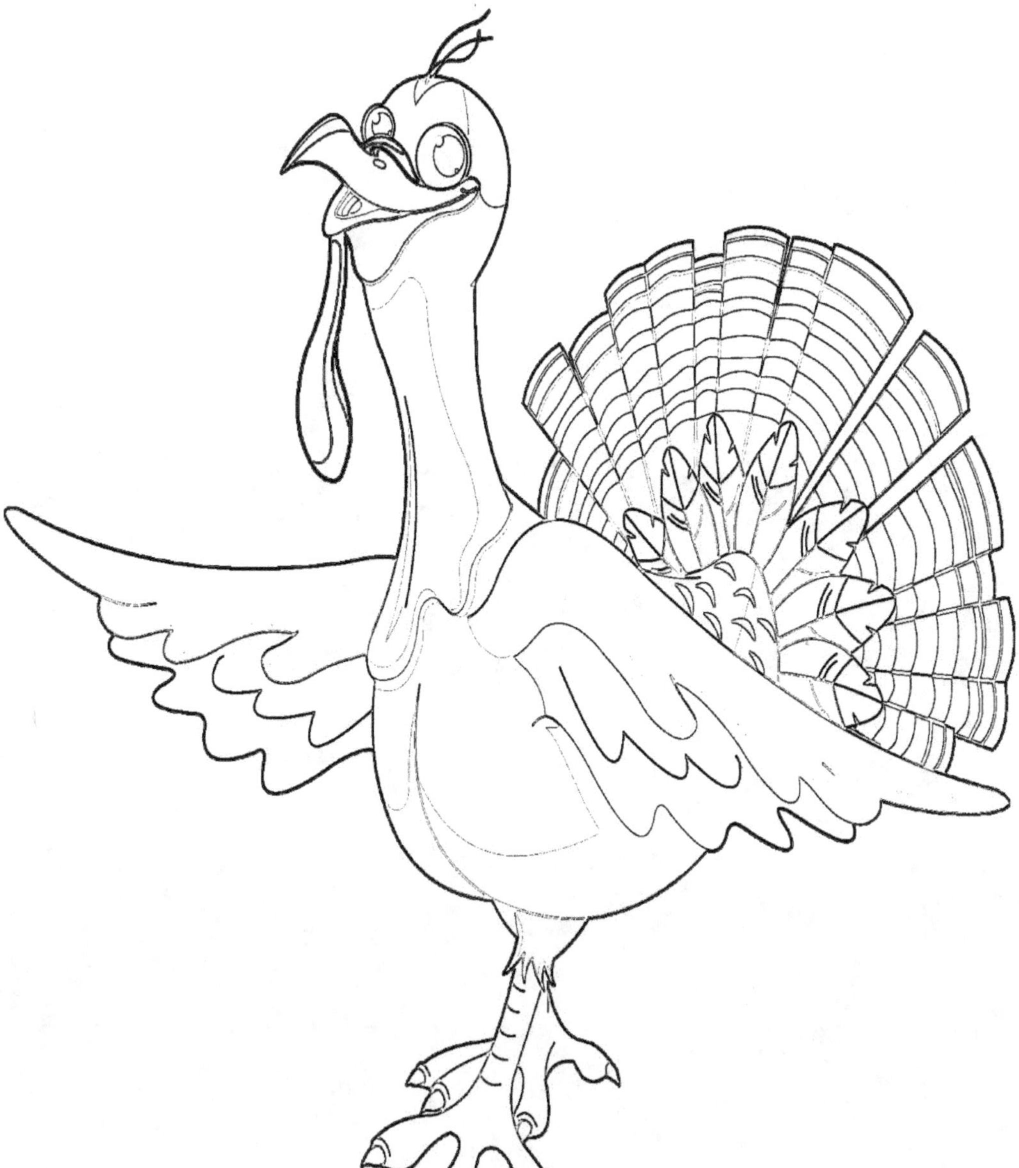

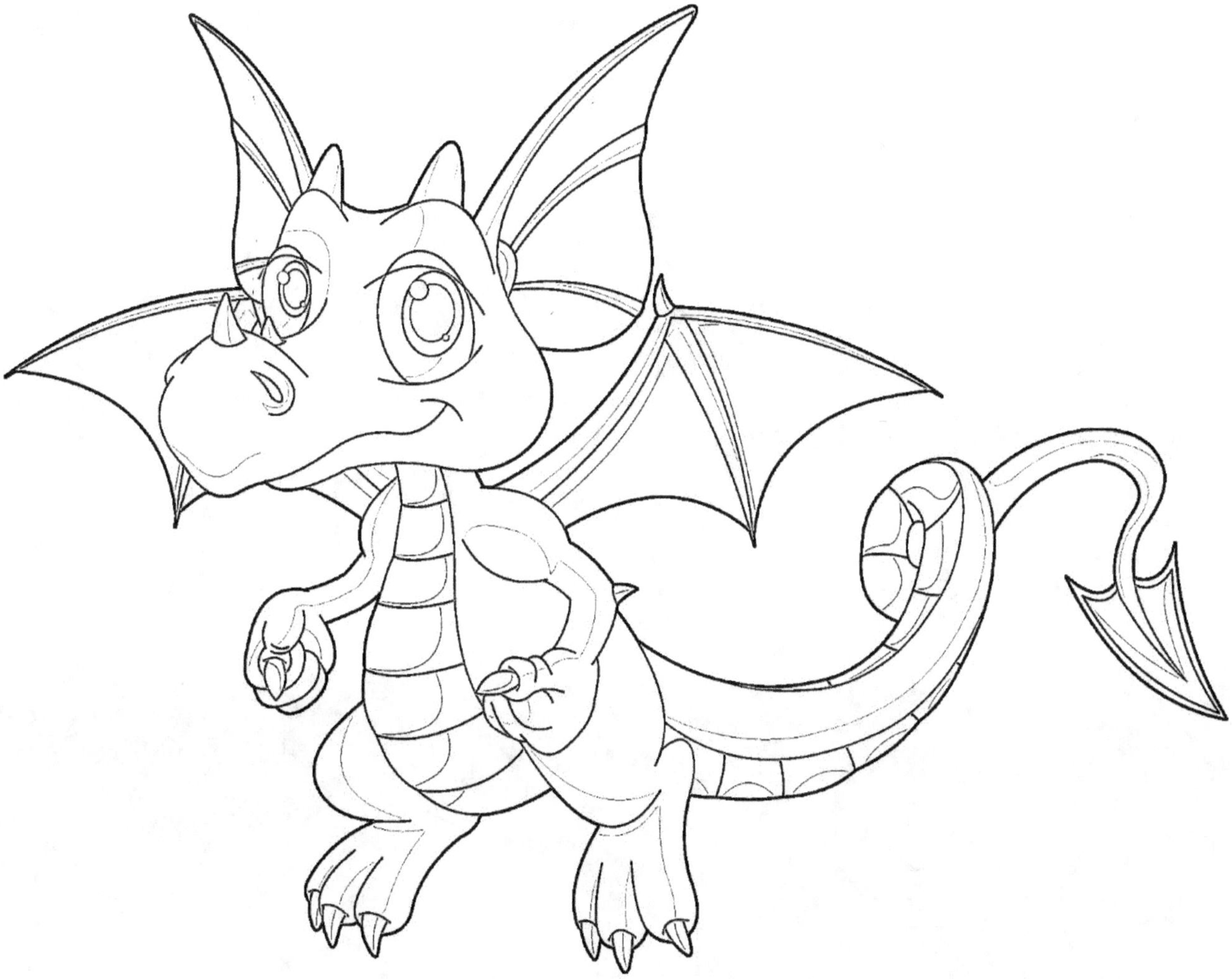

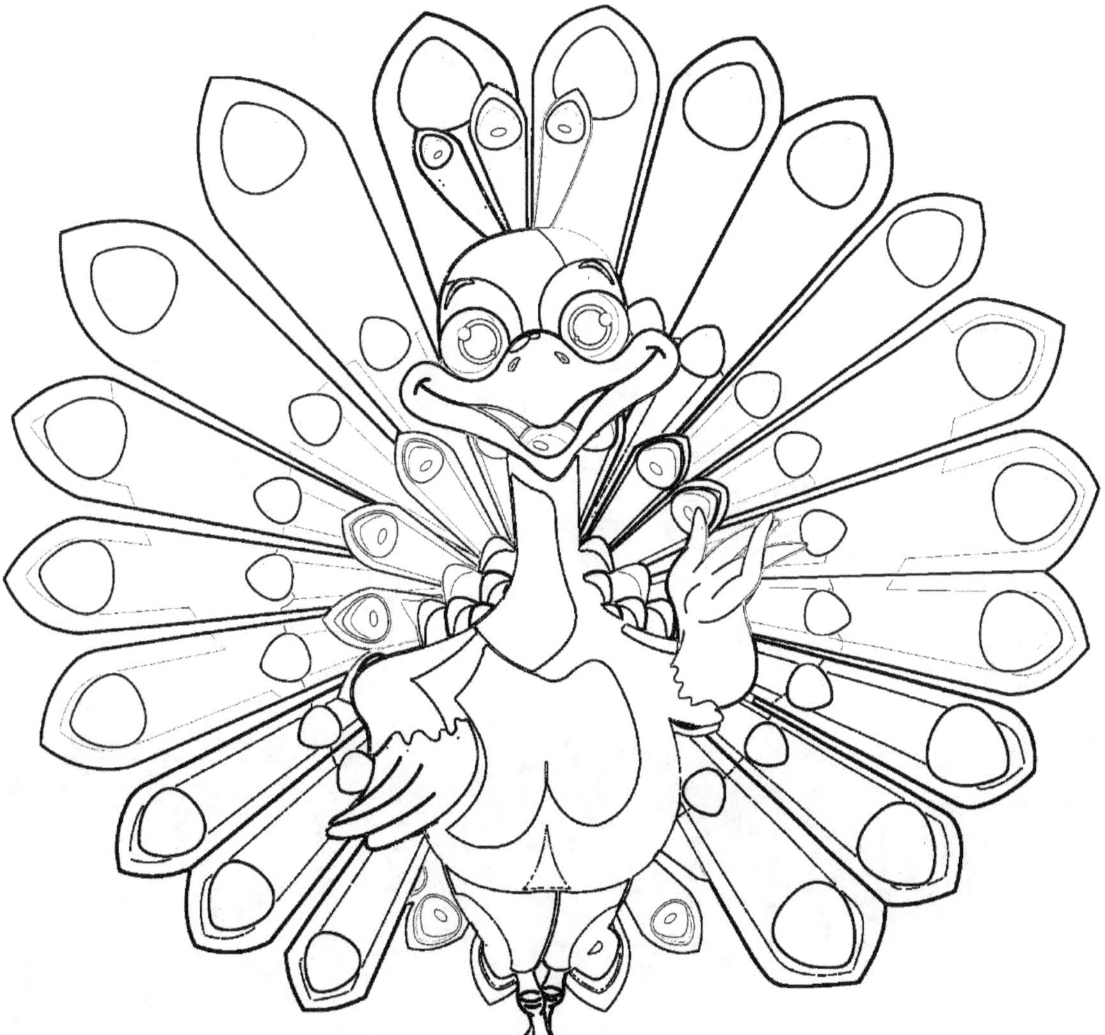

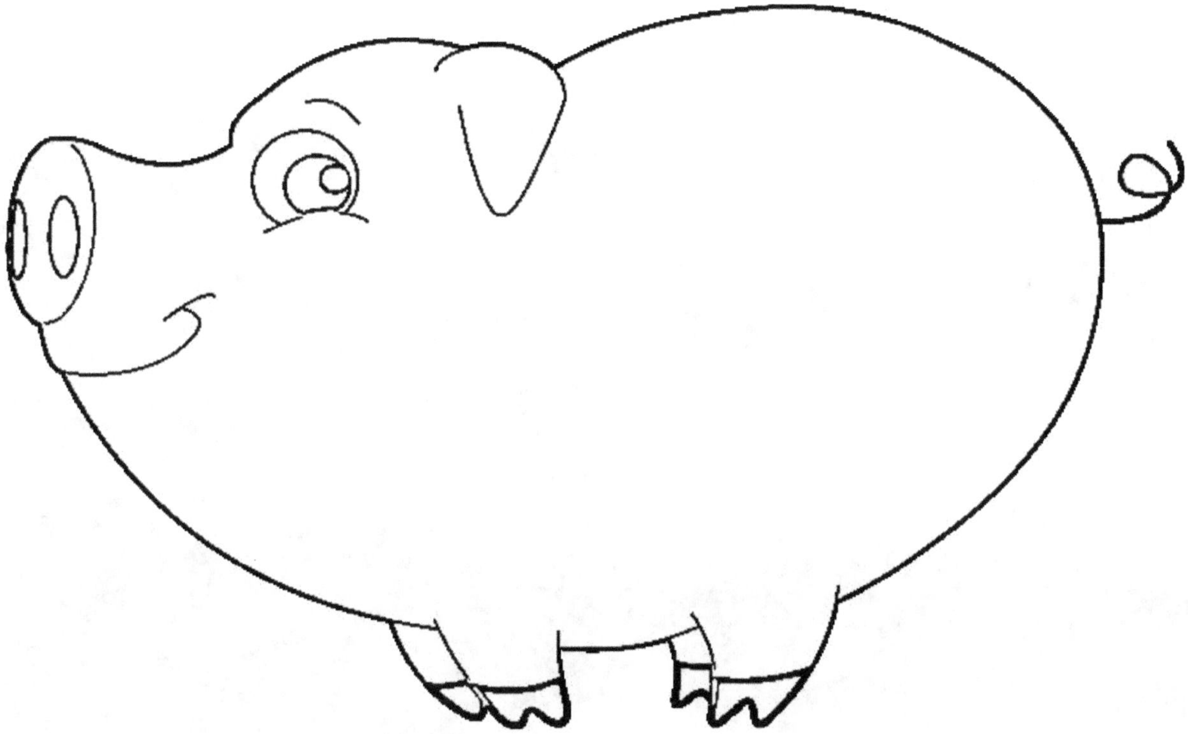

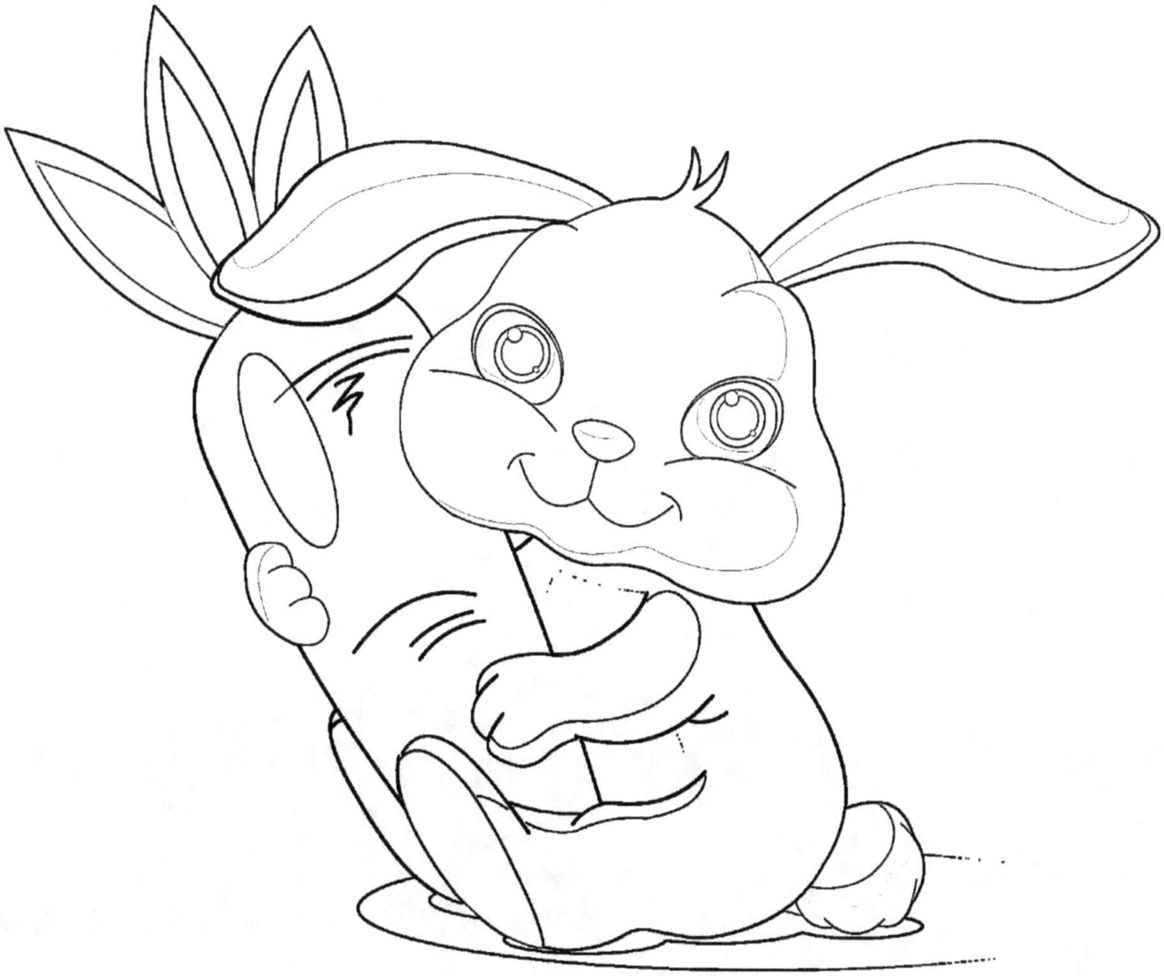

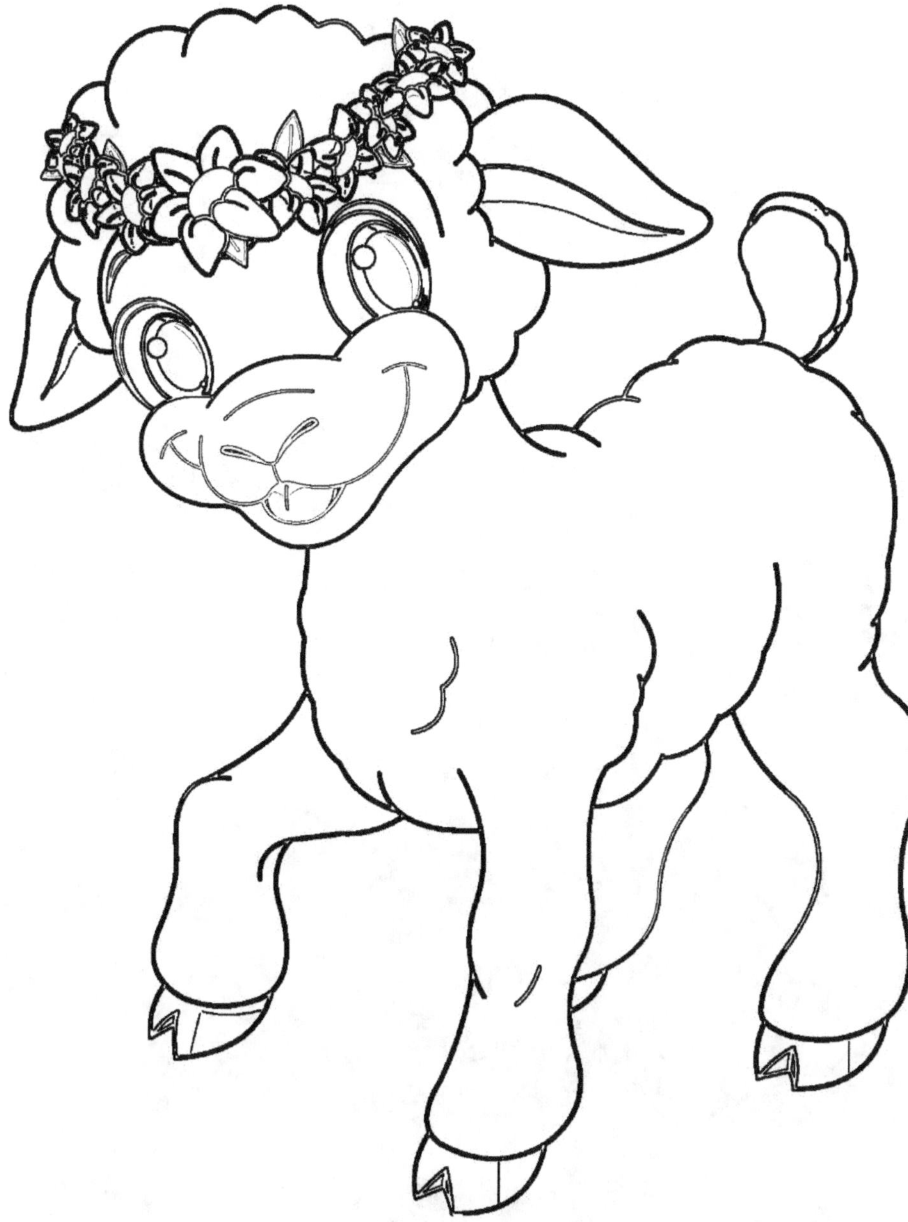

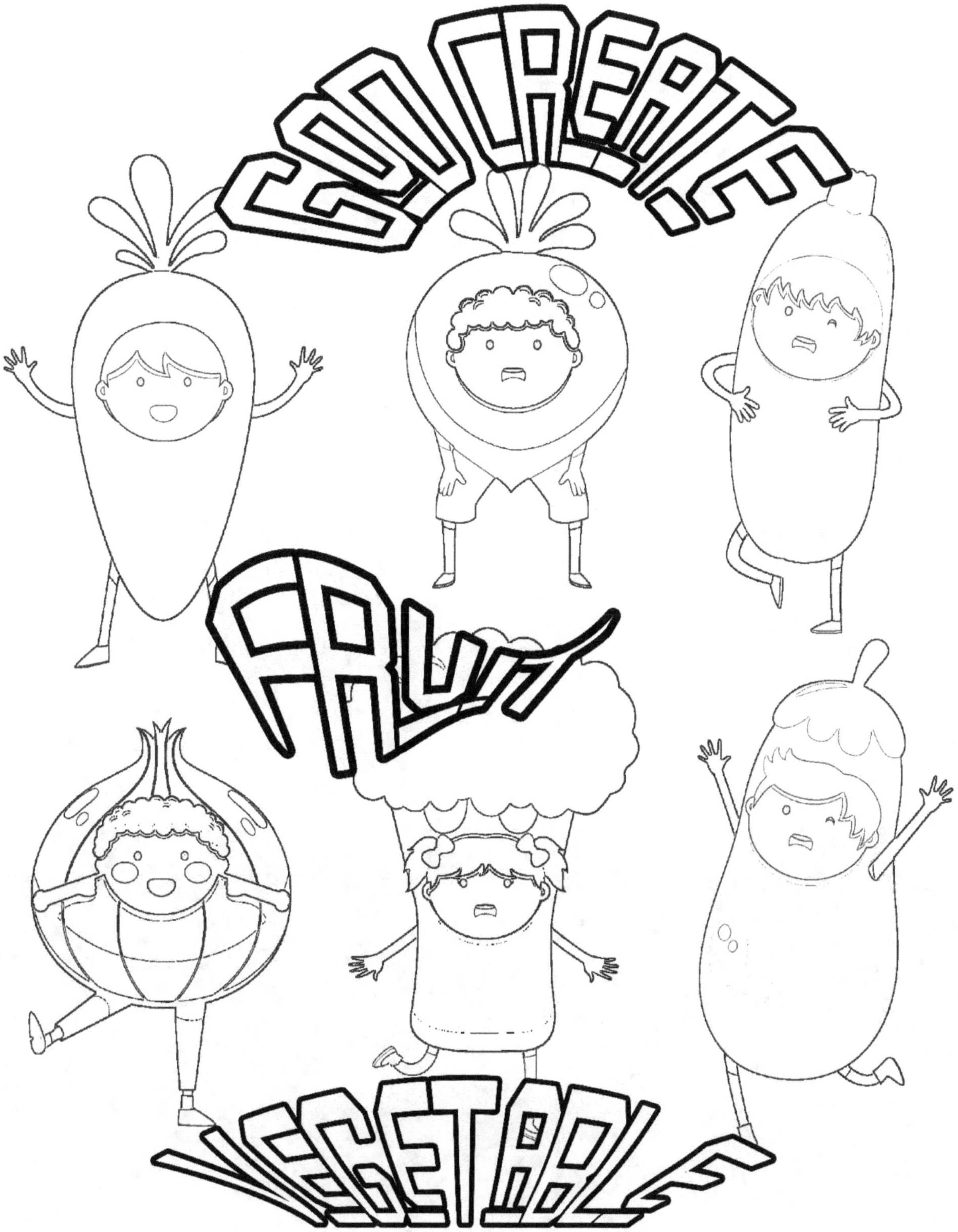
GOD CREATE
FRUIT
VEGETABLE

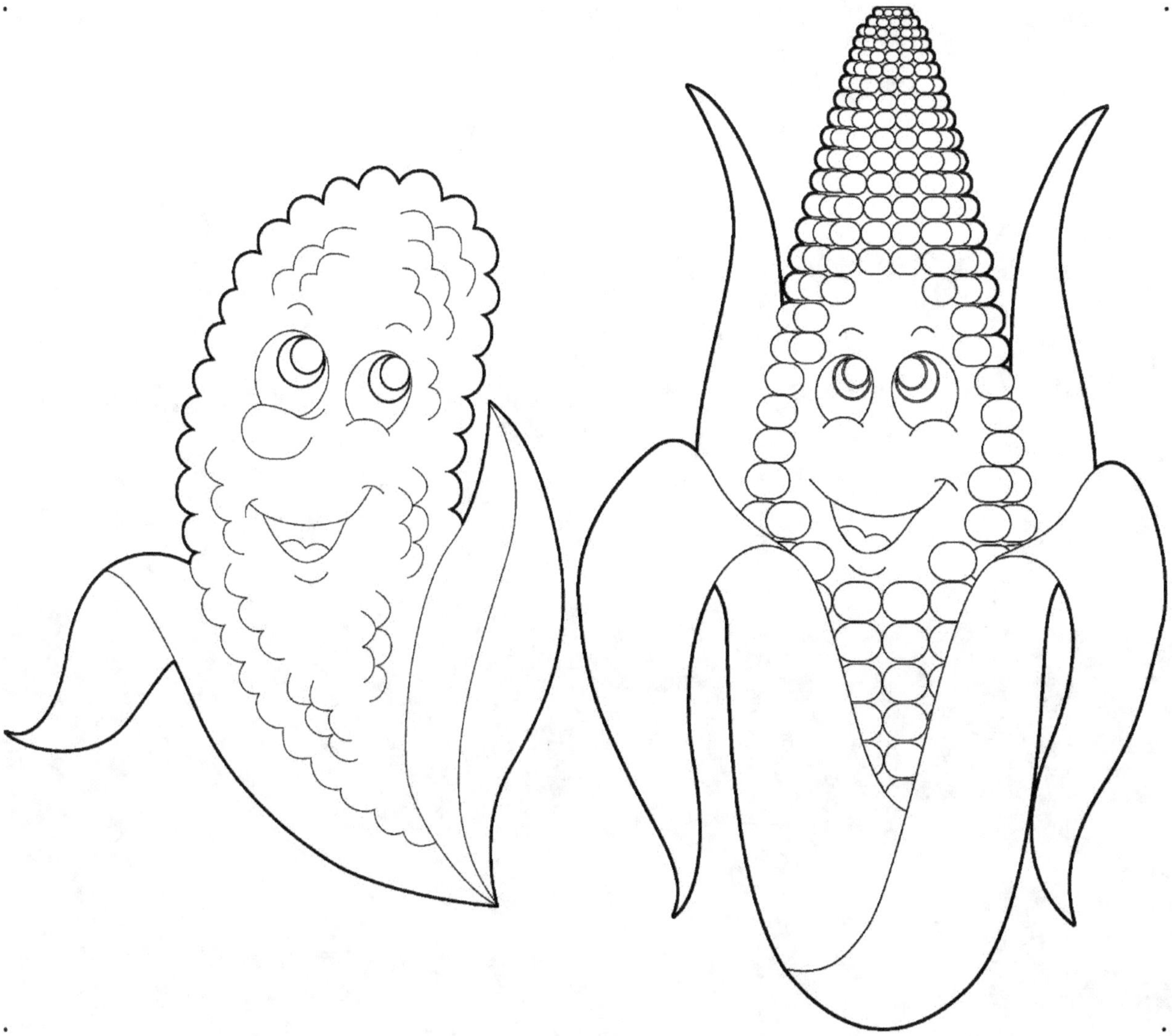

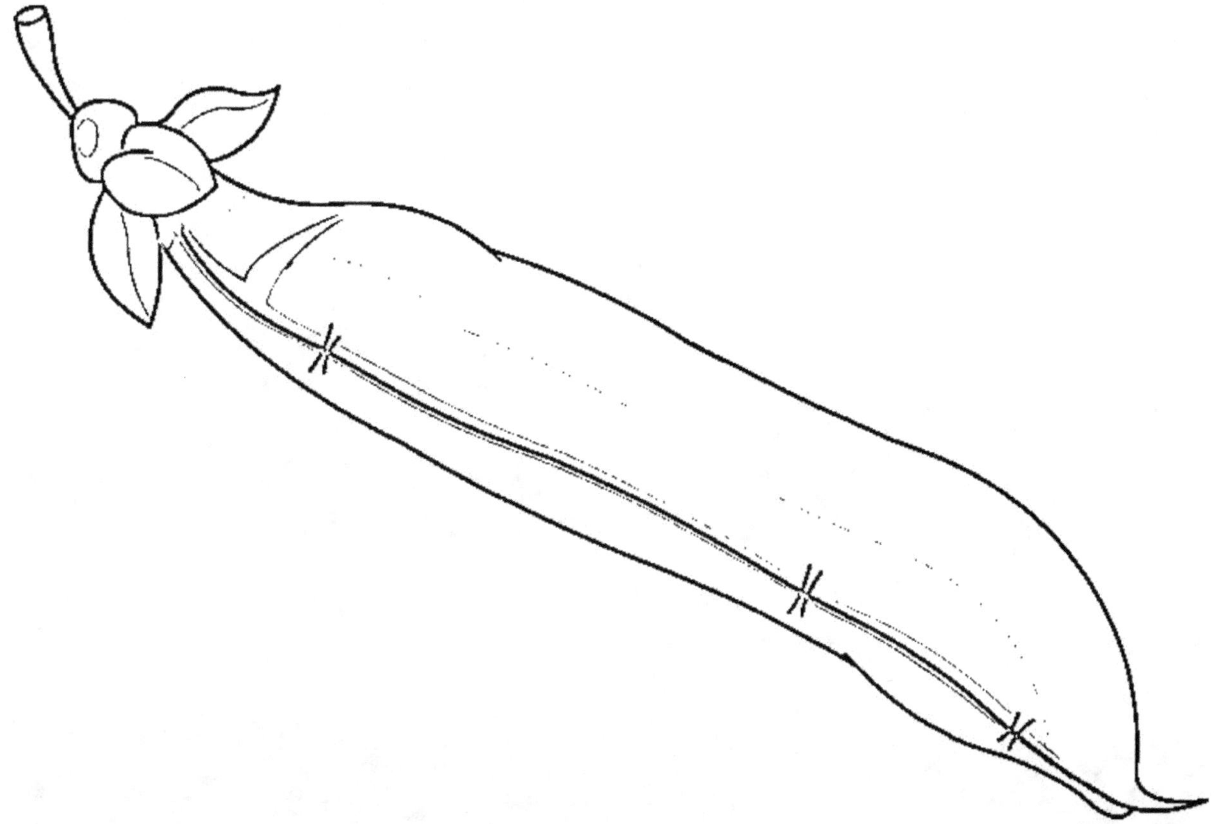

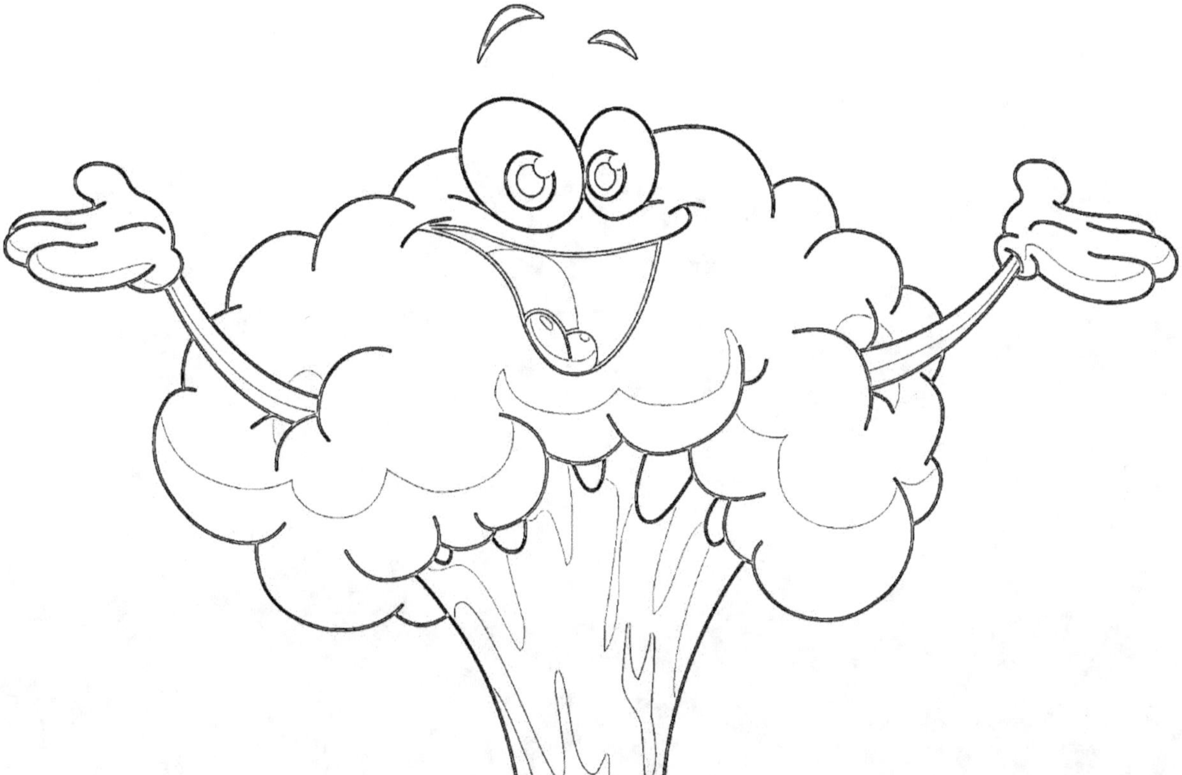

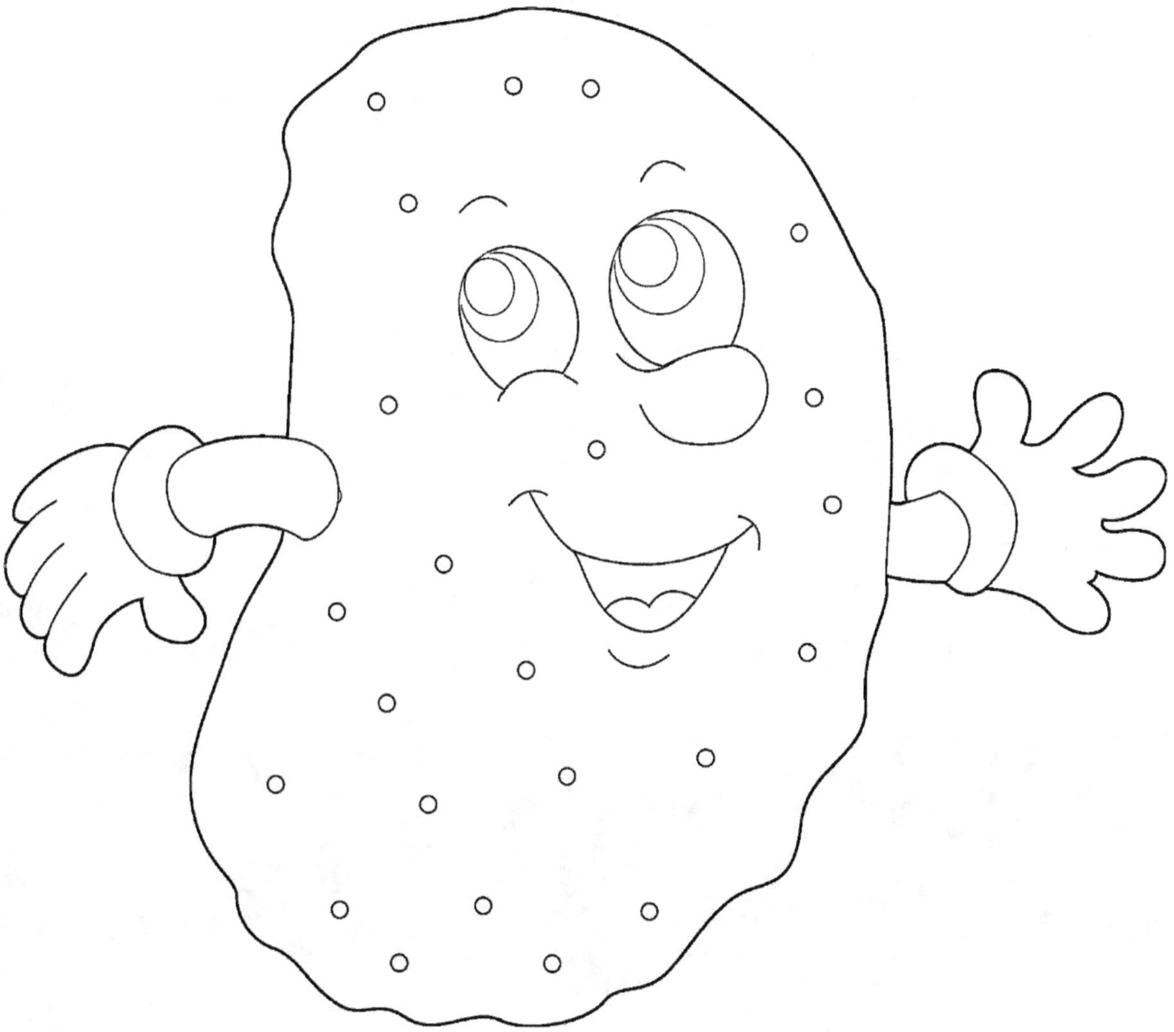

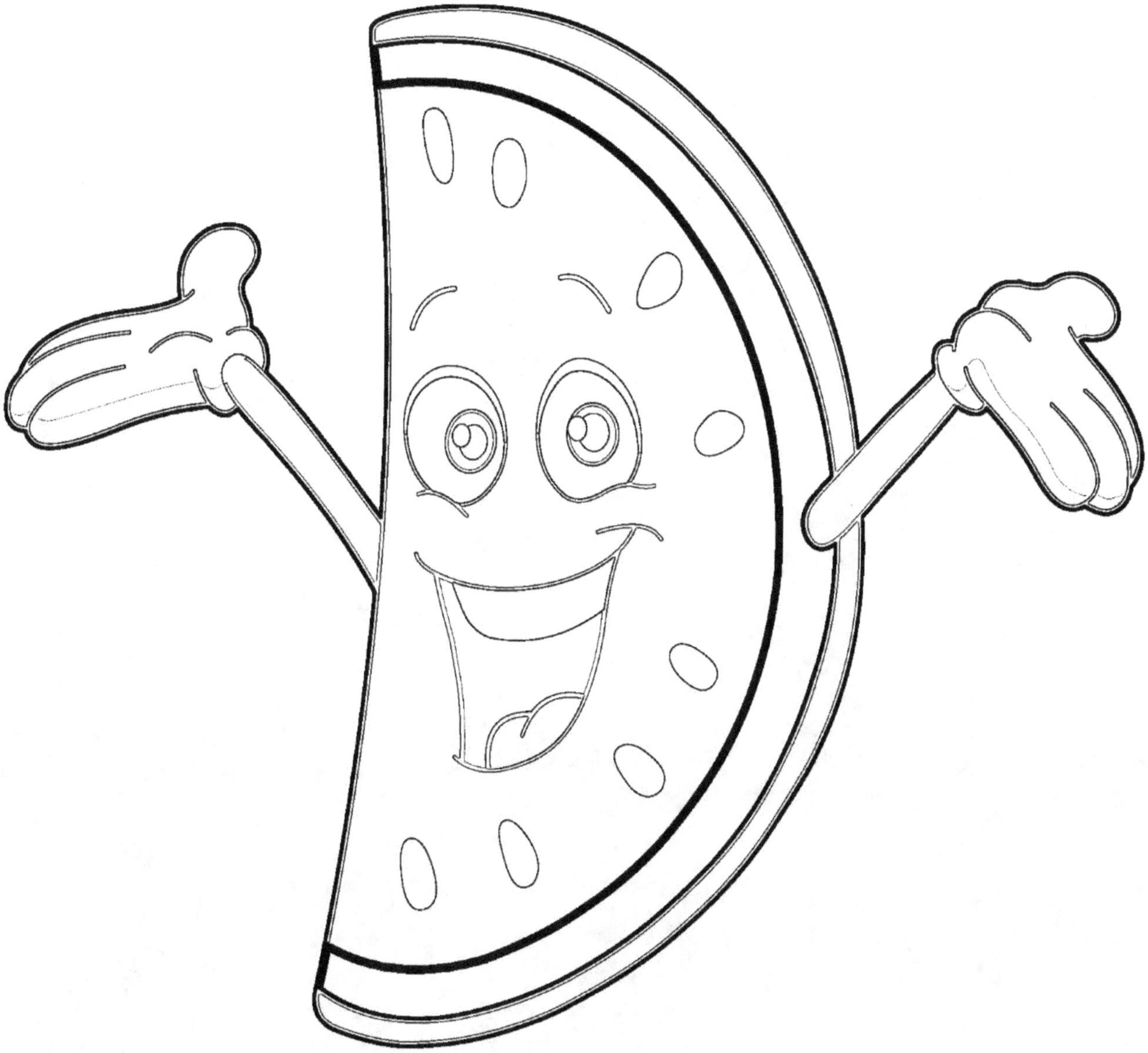

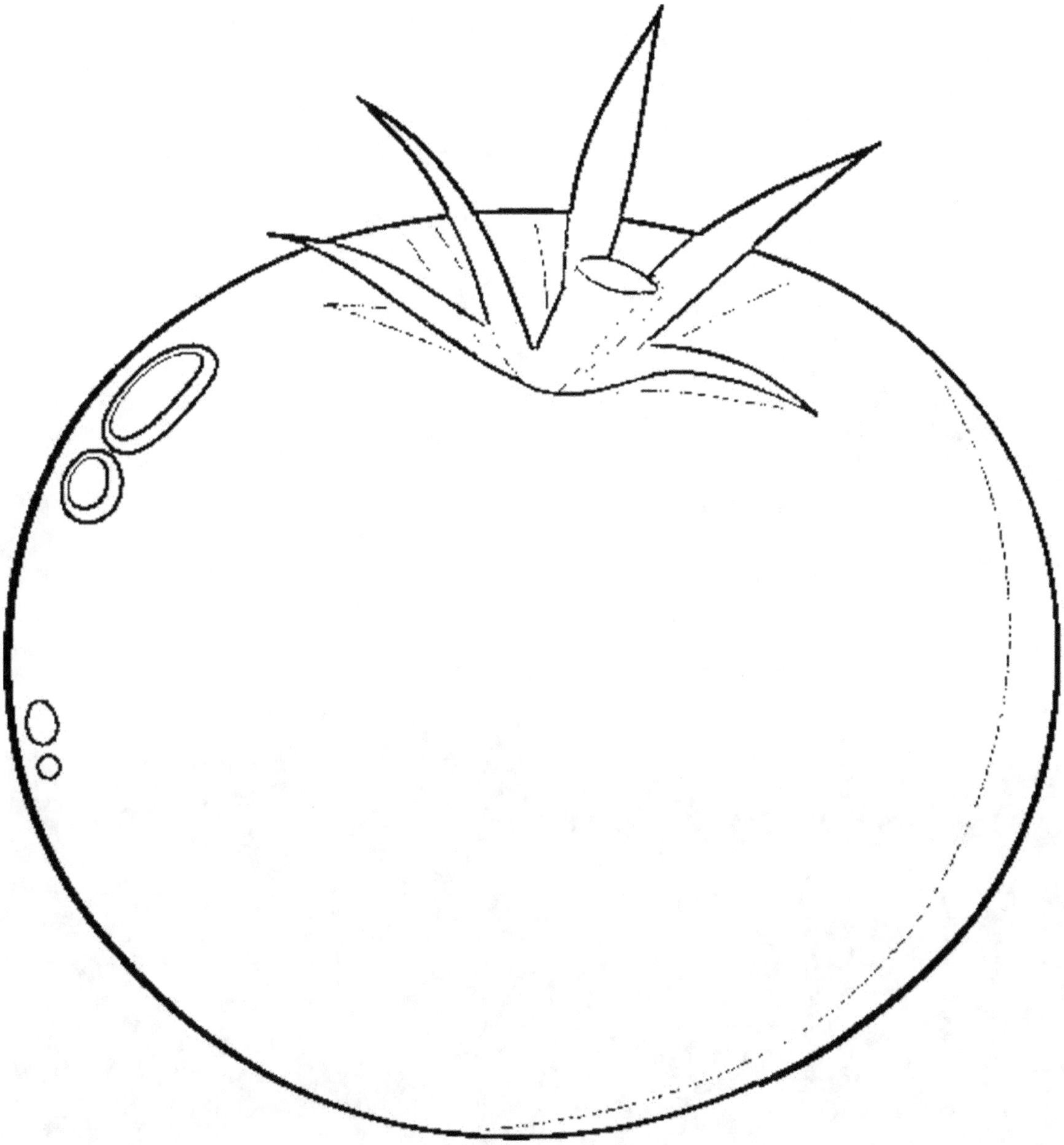

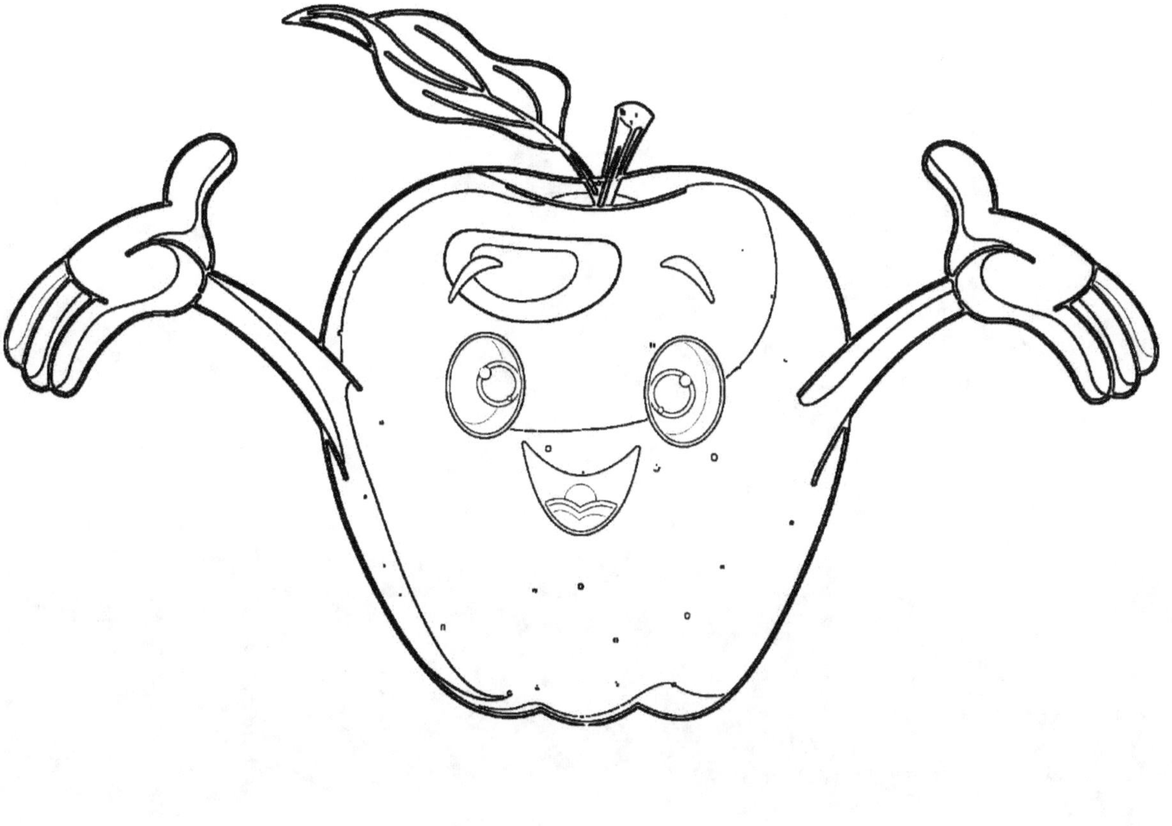

GOD CREATE ALL THINGS

GOD

OUR CREATOR

www.ingramcontent.com/pod-product-compliance
Lightning Source LLC
Chambersburg PA
CBHW081753170526
45167CB00009B/4019
9781543098242